The Clerk's Tale

The Clerk's Tale

Poems

Spencer Reece

A Mariner Original

HOUGHTON MIFFLIN COMPANY

BOSTON NEW YORK

2004

For information about permission to reproduce selections from this book, write to Permissions, Houghton Mifflin Company, 215 Park Avenue South, New York, New York 10003.

Visit our Web site: www.houghtonmifflinbooks.com.

Library of Congress Cataloging-in-Publication Data
Reece, Spencer.
The clerk's tale : poems / Spencer Reece.
p.   cm.
ISBN 0-618-42254-4
I. Title.
PS3618.E4354C58   2004
811'.6 — dc22   2003067577

Printed in the United States of America

Book design by Lisa Diercks
Typeset in Clifford Eighteen (FontShop).

WOZ 10 9 8 7 6 5 4 3

Grateful acknowledgment is made to the following publications, where some of these poems first appeared: *Boulevard*, "The Snake" and "The Elephant"; *Dandelion* (Canada), "The Frog"; *Imago* (Australia), "Interior"; *Negative Capability*, "Ghazals for Spring"; *Painted Bride Quarterly*, "Winter Scene"; *Poetry Wales* (Britain), "Fugue"; *New Welsh Review* (Britain), "Chrysanthemums"; *The New Yorker*, "The Clerk's Tale"; and *Seeds*, "Portofino," "Politics," and "Easter."

"The Clerk's Tale" was a semifinalist for *E: The Emily Dickinson Award Anthology*. "Autumn Song" was published in *Nimrod* as a semifinalist for the *Nimrod*/Hardman Pablo Neruda Poetry Award.

Grateful acknowledgment is also made to the Minnesota State Arts Board and the National Endowment for the Arts for a fellowship awarded during the writing of this book.

This book is dedicated to

Durell Goucher Hawthorne, Jr.
(1930–2003)

and

Elizabeth Anne Seibert
(1972–2000)

with gratitude and love.

Contents

Clarissa had a theory in those days — they had heaps of theories, always theories, as young people have. It was to explain the feeling they had of dissatisfaction; not knowing people; not being known. For how could they know each other? You met every day; then not for six months, or years. It was unsatisfactory, they agreed, how little one knew people. But she said, sitting on the bus going up Shaftesbury Avenue, she felt herself everywhere; not "here, here, here," and she tapped the back of the seat; but everywhere. She was all that. So that to know her, or anyone, one must seek out the people who completed them; even the places.

— Virginia Woolf, *Mrs. Dalloway*

Foreword

Chaucer's *The Clerk's Tale* tells the story of a marriage: the Marquis Walter marries the peasant girl Griselda, after exacting from her a vow of obedience which he proceeds ruthlessly to test. Griselda's radiant compliance makes of the tale a parable of virtue which, in Judeo-Christian tradition, flourishes in conditions of powerlessness. The tale is a problem for many contemporary readers, possibly because virtue unconvincingly disarms brutality, possibly because modern thinking is not inclined to equate moral virtue with obedience and patience, preferring, as its standard, action and protest.

Spencer Reece's extraordinary first book is no more a strict retelling of Chaucer's tale than his ghazals are strict ghazals. Chaucer survives as resonance and parallel; for all its shimmering ironies, this clerk's tale unfolds with an oddly objective, stoic clarity; its yearning toward goodness and understanding of fortitude suggest, but do not paraphrase, Griselda. And it begins, like Chaucer's narrative, with the request for a vow:

> Promise me you will not forget Portofino.
> Promise me you will find the trompe l'oeil
> on the bedroom walls at the Splendido.
> The walls make a scene you cannot enter.
>
> Perhaps then you will comprehend this longing
> for permanence I often mentioned to you . . .

Reece's mastery of tone and diction, his unobtrusive wit, show themselves in the exquisite disjunction between "permanence" and "often mentioned." "Promise me you will not forget": the fundamental human plea for corroboration. In this case, the promise, given, binds the beloved to the lover, the reader to the poet. The common referent is Portofino, not the place merely, but what was felt there, what was intimated there. What sustains the beautiful is loss: as the property of memory, the beautiful is elevated to that permanence and durability experienced, in perception, as its central attribute. Memory corrects time; in Portofino, infinite space turned into a wall; the eye was fooled, the illusory taken for the real.

Reece's longing for permanence is rooted in a profound sense of the provisional nature of all human arrangements and a corresponding perception of an ideal. The scene "you cannot enter," the world denied, recurs. This same hunger for permanence disposes him to find security in ritual and repetition; when the clerk, in the title poem, tells us "Mostly I talk of rep ties and bow ties, / of full-Windsor knots and half-Windsor knots," he is not speaking in frustration. The mall is, in its way, a retreat; the fact that nothing happens here that has not happened before induces, within the clerks' brotherhood of service, a nearly monastic composure. Medieval obedience has modulated into the clerks' prescribed patter and repetitive tasks; in the mall itself "the light is bright and artificial, / yet not dissimilar to that found in a Gothic cathedral."

Its light touch and connoisseur's passion for surface notwithstanding, this is a book of deprivations and closures, each somehow graver than the external sign suggests. Expansive description is sealed off in terse sentences: houses are sold, dogs are given away. Against these cumulative finalities, the dream of permanence makes an alternative or corrective. And beauty, especially remembered beauty, which is insulated against erosion, functions in these poems like a promise: it holds the self firm in the face of crushing solitude and transience.

I say "self" (in Reece's wonderful phrase, that "brochure of needs"), but these poems are filled with acts of unforgettable portraiture and complex social observation. Spencer Reece has something of Bishop's passion for detail, her scrupulousness, something of Lowell's genius for fixing character in gesture (like Lowell, he also chooses props brilliantly); the wild, inexhaustible fertility of his comparisons is, though, without exact antecedent, except perhaps in the similes and metaphors of children, to which Reece adds unique resources of vocabulary. Nowhere are these characteristics more striking than in the three major sequences that give this collection its weight and substance. By turns harrowing, comic, poignant, each in its own manner combines detached, elaborate refinements of scrutiny with an eerily skittish mobility of focus, so that the poems both see deeply and move nervously, like an animal in panic. It is an effect I have never quite seen before, half cocktail party, half passion play. The somnambulistic, corrosive violence of "Florida Ghazals," its sense of grief beyond remedy, give to the surrounding poems an air of quiet heroism and deep suffering. The poem builds slowly, incrementally:

Consider the teenage boy again. His locked room is a diorama of loneliness.
He bucks his hips until his hurricanes of desire are arrested. Then comes a
    deep silence.

Weather. Weather. How's the weather?
When I speak of the weather, is it because I cannot speak of my days spent in
the nuthouse?

Juan sinks into the swamp thick with processed excrement.
Nude paper ladies sink him like cement, silencing him.

The men in the gym slow down their repetitions, their biceps grow; they are
silent in their strength.
When does silence go from being an asset to being a liability?

The parallel isolations never fuse; isolation, for Reece, is plural, social. Rather there
is introduced, gradually, an event more absolute, more devastating. What would be
in another poet an occasion for moralizing, a catalyst for change, is here merely another horror, absorbed into the swamp.

The long poems change the scale of this art, but Reece's breadth and precision
of gaze, his often fizzy inventiveness, are everywhere apparent, emblems of humanity and generosity. "Everyone's a fugitive," he tells us. "Everyone." We meet many
in these pages:

There was a yacht club meeting every summer
with a cannon that went off — *baboom!*
Women arrived in their thin Talbots belts,
carrying wicker purses shaped like paint cans
with whalebone carvings fastened on top,
resembling the hardened excrement seagulls drop.
Occasionally the purses would open,
albeit reluctantly, like safe-deposit boxes.

Or, in the title poem:

. . . Our hours are long. Our backs bent.
We are more gracious than English royalty.
We dart amongst the aisles tall as hedgerows.
Watch us fade into the merchandise.
How we set up and take apart mannequins

as if we were performing autopsies.
A naked body, without pretense, is of no use.

Like Lautrec's drawings: so much *world* in so few lines!

We do not expect virtuosity as the outward form of soul-making, nor do we associate generosity and humanity with such sophistication of means, such polished intelligence. Like all genuinely new work, Spencer Reece's compels a reevaluation of the possible. Much life has gone into the making of this art, much patient craft. And intelligence that postulates the cost of self-preservation, which is spontaneity:

> I remember the ponies in the distance.
> I remember you talked of a war, no, two wars, a failed marriage —
> discreetly, without force of grandeur.
> This was before they amputated your leg, before the stroke.
> You rolled your *r*'s, spoke of Oxford,
> recalled driving in the Quaker ambulance unit in China,
> where you saw an oil drum filled with severed limbs.
> Pleased to have your approval, I rarely spoke.
> You were like a father to me and I was grateful.
> I remember the ponies behind the fence, muscular,
> breathing, how they worried the grass.
> The ponies said: *This day astounds us. The field is green.*
> *We love nothing better than space and more space.*
> Ah, they knew what I needed to know.
> They lived in their bodies.
> If the ponies wanted to kiss, they kissed.

Artless naturalness is one thing in the field and quite another on the page, where its simulation tends to produce self-congratulatory tedium. Among the triumphs of *The Clerk's Tale* is this tone, so supple, so deft, so capable of simultaneous refinements and ironies as to seem not a tone, not an effect of art, but the truth.

How are we to master suffering? Over and over, the poems in *The Clerk's Tale* discover in modesty a discipline by which the desire to affirm can overcome repeated disappointment that threatens to become withdrawal or despair. They take solace in simple decency; they admire dignity, as they admire the natural forms in which spontaneity survives. But Reece's art is not modest (as it is not sentimental or pious). By some bizarre alchemy, modesty of expectation fuels in this poet a profound capacity for wonder — at nature, at language, at human beauty and bravery, at vistas and interiors. I felt, reading this book, a sense of Herbert's luminous simplicities somehow crossed with Anne Carson's caustic epigrammatic brilliance and Merrill's perfect pitch. An odd sensation, as though the ingenious confectioner were also the postulant. I do not know a contemporary book in which poems so dazzlingly entertaining contain, tacitly, such deep sorrow.

"The frankly marvelous has not always been in disrepute," James Sledd remarks in his discussion of Chaucer's Griselda. I felt emanating from Spencer Reece's work a sense of immanence that belongs more commonly to religious passion; it is a great thing to have it again in art:

When the ficus beyond the grillwork darkens,
when the rind cools down on the lime,
when we sit here for a long time,
when we feel ourselves found,
. . . we will turn at last,
we will admire the evening's fading clues,
uncertain of what the dark portends
as another season ends
and the fabulous visitors depart in luxury cars,
we will savor the sharp light from the summer stars,
we will rejoice in the fronds tintinnabulating down these empty streets,
these beautiful streets with all these beautiful names —
Kings, Algoma, Via Bellaria, Clarendon, Via Vizcaya,
Via Del Mar, El Vedado, Banyan, El Brillo, El Bravo, Via Marina.

LOUISE GLÜCK

Portofino

Promise me you will not forget Portofino.
Promise me you will find the trompe l'oeil
on the bedroom walls at the Splendido.
The walls make a scene you cannot enter.

Perhaps then you will comprehend this longing
for permanence I often mentioned to you.
Across the harbor? A yellow church. A cliff.
Promise me you will witness the day diminish.

And when the roofs darken, when the stars drift
until they shatter on the sea's finish,
you will know what I told you is true
when I said abandonment is beautiful.

The Clerk's Tale

I am thirty-three and working in an expensive clothier,
selling suits to men I call "Sir."
These men are muscled, groomed and cropped—
with wives and families that grow exponentially.
Mostly I talk of rep ties and bow ties,
of full-Windsor knots and half-Windsor knots,
of tattersall, French cuff, and English spread collars,
of foulards, neats, and internationals,
of pincord, houndstooth, nailhead, and sharkskin.
I often wear a blue pin-striped suit.
My hair recedes and is going gray at the temples.
On my cheeks there are a few pimples.
For my terrible eyesight, horn-rimmed spectacles.
One of my fellow-workers is an old homosexual
who works hard and wears bracelets with jewels.
No one can rival his commission checks.
On his break he smokes a Benson & Hedges cigarette,
puffing expectantly as a Hollywood starlet.
He has carefully applied a layer of Clinique bronzer
to enhance the tan on his face and neck.
His hair is gone except for a few strands
which are combed across his scalp.
He examines his manicured lacquered nails.
I admire his studied attention to details:
his tie stuck to his shirt with masking tape,
his teeth capped, his breath mint in place.
The old homosexual and I laugh in the back
over a coarse joke involving an octopus.
Our banter is staccato, staged and close
like those "Spanish Dances" by Granados.

I sometimes feel we are in a musical —
gossiping backstage between our numbers.
He drags deeply on his cigarette.
Most of his life is over.
Often he refers to himself as "an old faggot."
He does this bemusedly, yet timidly.
I know why he does this.
 He does this because his acceptance is finally complete —
and complete acceptance is always
bittersweet. Our hours are long. Our backs bent.
We are more gracious than English royalty.
We dart amongst the aisles tall as hedgerows.
Watch us fade into the merchandise.
How we set up and take apart mannequins
as if we were performing autopsies.
A naked body, without pretense, is of no use.
It grows late.
I hear the front metal gate close down.
We begin folding the ties correctly according to color.
The shirts — Oxfords, broadcloths, pinpoints —
must be sized, stacked, or rehashed.
The old homosexual removes his right shoe,
allowing his gigantic bunion to swell.
There is the sound of cash being counted —
coins clinking, bills swishing, numbers whispered —
One, two, three, four, five, six, seven . . .
We are changed when the transactions are done —
older, dirtier, dwarfed.
A few late customers gawk in at us.
We say nothing. Our silence will not be breached.
The lights go off, one by one —
the dressing room lights, the mirror lights.
Then it is very late. How late? Eleven?
We move to the gate. It goes up.
The gate's grating checkers our cheeks.
This is the Mall of America.

The light is bright and artificial,
yet not dissimilar to that found in a Gothic cathedral.
You must travel down the long hallways to the exits
before you encounter natural light.
One final formality: the manager checks our bags.
The old homosexual reaches into his over-the-shoulder leather bag —
the one he bought on his European travels
with his companion of many years.
He finds a stick of lip balm and applies it to his lips
liberally, as if shellacking them.
Then he inserts one last breath mint
and offers one to me. The gesture is fraternal
and occurs between us many times.
At last, we bid each other good night.
I watch him fade into the many-tiered parking lot,
where the thousands of cars have come
and are now gone. This is how our day ends.
This is how our day always ends.
Sometimes snow falls like rice.
See us take to our dimly lit exits,
disappearing into the cities of Minneapolis and St. Paul;
Minneapolis is sleek and St. Paul,
named after the man who had to be shown,
is smaller, older, and somewhat withdrawn.
Behind us, the moon pauses over the vast egg-like dome of the mall.
See us loosening our ties among you.
We are alone.
There is no longer any need to express ourselves.

Chiaroscuro

for Rocco and Jennifer Marcello on the occasion of their wedding

When the ficus beyond the grillwork darkens,
when the rind cools down on the lime,
when we sit here a long time,
when we feel ourselves found,
when the red tile roofs deepen to brown,
when the exhausted beach fires with blues,
when the hush of the waves reminds us of regrets,
when the tides overtake the shore,
when we begin to place God in our sentences more,
we will turn at last,
we will admire the evening's fading clues,
uncertain of what the dark portends
as another season ends
and the fabulous visitors depart in luxury cars,
we will savor the sharp light from the summer stars,
we will rejoice in the fronds tintinnabulating down these empty streets,
these beautiful streets with all these beautiful names —
Kings, Algoma, Via Bellaria, Clarendon, Via Vizcaya,
Via Del Mar, El Vedado, Banyan, El Brillo, El Bravo, Via Marina.

A Bestiary

for Tina Howe and Norman Levy

i. The Snake

I move through the meadow
in pieces. I am a mirror

thrown down, a tuxedo
undone. My scales

shatter into arpeggios.
I am all

you cannot marry.
All by myself,

with my Scheherazadey body,
I will kiss and multiply,

kiss and multiply.

ii. The Frog

My throat rings.
My strong tongue
the pond's clock.

In my season
of teen fame,
I'm pimpleless.

Although young,
I'm nearly done.
Advance me quick.

iii. The Bat

My kisses map the dark.
I open myself —

a brochure of needs.
Wherever I go

I circle and do not
slaughter. My world

is spectacular
because I cannot see it.

iv. The Cat

I motor myself
and clean and clean.
Love bores me

and sex I never did
understand. Do you?
My lips traffic

in ruminations —
my skull a terrarium
of regrets. No.

I want no other life.

v. The Elephant

In my monk cell,
my trunk coils —
a crucifix
or a question mark.

Which one of you
unscrewed me
from the blue jungle
like a chandelier

and placed me here?

Tonight

You are being born. Feels good.
Something enormous kisses you.
Its eye surveys your revolutions.
Relaxed in your new nudity,

you work your labyrinthine ears,
those perfect disciples,
registering all that hums, ticks.
O you encyclopedia you,

you do not know what I know,
how blank the cold world can grow.
But let the addendums come later.
I listen to the dust from the city

gather on the necks of the saints
at the hospital's exits I exit.
And so I say to you yes you:
everyone's a fugitive. Everyone.

Then

I was a full-time house sitter. I had no title.
I lived in a farmhouse, on a small hill,
surrounded by 100 acres. All was still.
The fields were in a government program
that paid farmers to abandon them. Perfect.

I overlooked Union Lake, a small lake,
with a small ugly island in the middle —
a sort of mistake, a cluster of dead elms
encircled by marsh, resembling a smear
of oil paint left to congeal on a palette.

Pesticides farmers sprayed on their crops
over the years had drained into the lake
and made the water black, the fish shake.
About the family that built the house
I knew nothing. Built in 1865;

perhaps they came after the Civil War?
It was a simple house. Two stories.
Six rooms. Every wall crooked.
Before the house, Indians camped there.
If you listened you could hear them.

On Sunday afternoons in early June,
the sun would burnish the interiors.
Shafts of light fell across the rooms.
An old gray cat sparred his mote-swirls.
Up a tiny staircase, ladder steep,

I was often found, adrift, half asleep.
I forgot words, where I lived, my dreams.
Mirrors around the house, those streams,
ran out of gossip. The walls absorbed me.
There was every indication I was safe there.

Outside, children sang, sweetening the air —
Row, row, row your boat, gently down the stream.
Merrily, merrily, merrily, merrily, life is but a dream —
their fingers marrying each other with ease
as the dark built its scaffolding above the trees.

Peonies spoiled, dye ran from their centers.
Often the lawn was covered by a fine soft rain.
Days disappeared as quickly as they came.
The children receded. The moon rose.
Cows paused on the wild green plain

of all that land still left uncommercialized.
Three years I had there. Alone. At peace.
Often I awoke as the light began to cease.
The house breathed and shook like a lover
as I took for myself time needed to recover.

Chrysanthemums

When I am in the hospital there is this boy.
He is seventeen and has survived a circus fire.

His eye sockets are gouges.
The eyes themselves are like slugs

inching. His fingers are missing,
the stumps are black.

When the nurse undoes his gauze bandages,
his mouth collapses.

The shower room is soundproofed
so we cannot hear the screams

when they debride him.
The hours pass: quick, then slow.

Outside my window —
the chrysanthemums,

their petals yellow and scalloped as woodcuts.

Autumn Song

The muscular sky of Minnesota is more than I can fathom,
     full of salmon-colored promises of just how expansive love can be
at a time like this where the growing slow hunger of fall hushes
     and sounds in the footsteps of squirrels whirling like dervishes
and in the slopping slough-sound of mad cows crazy in love.
     The human being naked in love is lovelier in the autumn dusk
than on a summer's day. Most blowhards lead you to believe

romance hangs itself most astoundingly in the summertime,
     but I am here to say fall is lovelier still for falling in love,
for a love that stills the heart, that rustles our dust with good news —
     when the maple sweats and saps at the corners of his mouth
and when the oak shakes his leaves like a thousand horseshoes
     is the time my heart bangs with barn-joy and I breathe in the subtle
approbation of death coming as I recognize the Byzantine look

of the trees emptying themselves of themselves. The leaves fall
     like leaflets in a relentless war and the architecture of skeletons
becomes more and more apparent and the water wavers, the water cracks,
     and everywhere this upturned look, the look of one last kiss,
and on such a night as this, I feel dignity, I feel survival; in the nude
     descent of the earth shedding its sweat, its passion, my breath,
my shimmering cargo, is eager to dawn and break free from its hold.

Midnight

I quite expect to end my life caring most for a place.

— E. M. Forster

Pine trees stir in a chorus of darkness.
The lake taps the shore as if to tell me something.
A light rain increases the abstractions, all edges blur.
Dark tilled fields stretch for miles.
The Midwest settles into my chest.
Colts bolt across untouched Dakota acres
alive with the cymbal-smash of affectionate caresses.
Farms, barns, somnolent cows, empty gravel roads and distant houses
make up the landscape I walk in, where once, a long time ago,
Indians slept and walked, dissolving into the shadows with tenderness.
On Andy Cleland's farm, the one closest to the lake,
where cattails flourish at the water's edge,
there is one huge hill, vacant of shrubbery.
I was told once it was an Indian burial mound
and that was why no tree or bush would grow on that hill.
All these years later and the hill is still bald,
whispering softly as the revolutions of the sea,
echoing with the mouths of the vanquished.
Sheep maraud across the hill's back,
exhilarated by the dirt smells born again by spring,
the wind haunted with the songs of comrades now gone.
The rest of this panorama is immense, dark, impenetrable, unstructured.
But if you look closely in the left-hand corner,
I can just be distinguished from the blue blue brilliance of all this land,

a tiny figure, no bigger than a grass blade, a shadow hugged by shadows,
heading home after a long walk nowhere,
encircled by a halo of rocks, trees, crops, rivers, clouds —
by every blessed thing conspiring together to save my life.

Winter Scene

Snow piles up around the house, thick as pillows.
No people. No music. No invitations.
Plowed roads diminish into tiny zinc strips.
Cold stars snail away.

From my gutters, icicles drop their sharp braids.
A squirrel quivers, useless as an old Band-Aid.
Asphyxiated rivers exact crazed smiles
that will not go down.

But there! A spot of color. My basset hound.
He inspects the snow like an astronomer
transfixed; registering his findings, he knows
no disappointment.

Soon I must leave this house, give the dog away.

Diminuendo

for Barney Bush

The heat of the Midwest night fills with the hush of elms
weeping in the bluest of shadows,
their limbs cavernous as Jesus' limbs must have been,
while two lovers liberate themselves in the grasses
and the vegetables converse in small support groups
about the catastrophe of their ensuing deaths
and the sky gushes and the lilies of the fields tremble
in the diminishing angle of hours when nursing homes buzz
and the aged fumble their way through halls
to a numb white oblivion like melancholy gondoliers
lumbering under the stars that bend to the effort of their groans,
and when the grandmothers of this universe,
who are the real professors of history, fall off their pillow-cliffs,
their bangled durable prayers howl through the night's inky branches,
their history blasts down the hard sidewalks,
and their wishes go more or less unobserved,
at 4 A.M. on a grainy morning in Northfield, Minnesota.

Ghazals for Spring

i

I've been waiting for the tulip bulbs, those necessary ambulances,
to come and sound the emergencies of the world. Nothing so far.

I've been thinking about a seventeen-year-old boy named Daryl who hanged
      himself in my high school;
The kids teased him awful; that was just before spring.

Trees write their autobiographies in circles every year,
pausing briefly each spring to weep over what they have written. I guess that's life.

March, 1945. Anne Frank dies in the concentration camp in Bergen-Belsen:
the sky birdless, soldiers bark and the world grows exceedingly dark.

Once I thought *I* was in love, the way you looked at me, but by spring
you'd left me with the lies that crawled in my heart, small worms.

Everybody lies, I guess, and usually it happens in spring,
when the sky plumes to a deep Jesusy blue.

The high school dances were the worst — the spring prom —
we twitched to rock music like sad viruses.

ii

Hours clot. Birds flap like passports.
Fields explode with temper tantrums. Here comes trouble.

My soul has drifted too long like a cloud, so come and heal me,
bring me to the dirt, let my pores ooze with the brine of discotheques.

Hey you! Come unto me! Let the meadow march into my mouth!
I'm due for a moist trembling emotion, don't you think? Well, don't you?

Yesterday evening the daffodil shoots swallowed the horizon like butter;
now we wait all day for the color of yellow to bubble in their throats.

Ouch! Enough with the arrows! I know spring is coming.
Still, I've had my fill of target practice, I've had my fill of flying babies.

Everywhere mouths worship the tickings of dangerous strangers.
All night the resurrected grasses are suitcased by cow-kisses.

Last fall the lilac bushes wrote very convincing suicide notes, however now
they appear to be staging a bawdy leg-kicking comeback: what to make of this?

iii

I've practically forgotten all about the people I hate. Amazing.
The weather warms and teases my fingertips, the stars seem almost tenable.

In college I lost my mind. At night, that awful first term, I hid in the theater,
a pale ghost, and watched rehearsals of *Cabaret* endlessly.

In February the stars are unrecognized, quiet, like longtime bachelors
they intractably orbit their way to an old flame's door and tentatively knock.

A deer zigzags down in the blue dawn and inspects the birch tree planted
just last year, reading it carefully, a stockbroker memorizing his newsprint.

Dostoyevsky believed you saw more ghosts the closer you came to dying.
I don't know. I sometimes think the older I get, the more ghosts I shed.

All winter our kitchen windows were blank pages, but today, with this crisp
new shivering, our windows fatten into enigmatic French prose poems.

I was eighteen. So much of what I knew was unfriendly, unlovely, but by spring
the campus burst forth with erotic-thighed maples that said, "Hey there!"

iv

At night, while the soccer team sleeps, their Adam's apples bounce athletically
from the meadows of their flesh, nothing but apricots.

1 A.M. In the mental hospital, hands fly, feet clomp. Coos and brays echo deep
in this dank labyrinth of rooms. These halls so similar to those in high schools.

2 A.M. Ruby and pearl fires pour down a hillside. Traffic? Or a distant circus, the rides
shutting down, the clowns and dwarfs smoking cigarettes with stark, jaded grimness?

In spring, the hands of the kindergartners are a stampede of dirty unicorns.
At breakfast, the lips of the kindergartners drip with volcanic rivulets of crushed stars.

One kiss in spring and your body transforms into a suburb of electricity.
You can't fool me, those *are* blue volts at your fingertips.

The animals are back and they're singing their prothalamia.
It's about time. And get a load of that forest! It's squirting filigree.

Look out! The melancholy cello is at it again, a grand ship,
moving his hips vigorously through the world: heartbreaker.

v

The moon peels back her scalp, spreads her iconography —
the dirt shines, mechanically kneading the hours of our deaths.

Tra la la la. Lovers fling their arms open like medicine cabinets,
offering their baptized scalps to fun new people like thesauruses.

The empty maple branch is a hawk claw snatching the caulked backs
of the stone-marked plots where the snow-cheeked dead still chant their names.

Freshman year, the pine trees reproached me, a chorus of frozen adults,
while the stars footnoted the sky like a zillion empty wedding rings.

The forest is nothing but Brechtian scaffolding.
All night I whistle and wait patiently for the revolution.

Angels follow their stage directions. Feverish trees celebrate their new moneys.
Corn trumpets its guts toward the sun's razors.

In the lake's basement vaults, rainbows hibernate, tossed-off mildewed accordions.
But don't worry. Under the muck, a musical starring the primary colors is in the works.

vi

The high school teasing is gone — the woofs, the oinks — only these unfenced vistas
to cradle where each morning mouths are propped open like old barn windows.

Lawns blush, here and there amongst the forest the lost spangles of dawn revelers.
Always after darkness, the applause, the paparazzi.

In *The Berlin Stories,* the woeful pompom sounds of war hew and blast the city's edges
as Christopher shivers, alone, under the stars, the crazy, abiding, ceaseless stars.

Churches pitch, rock, and eddy, small sailboats. In the town's chinks,
lovers crouch and hoo, squeezing and popping their nectars.

The oak leaf? A mystery novel the caterpillar reads with a microscope.
Elsewhere grasshoppers answer multiple-choice questions until they die.

Uh-huh, somewhere there exists someone with luxurious girth on a bed
with lace trimming who is ready to torpedo your entire life. Ready your suitcases.

Dear Diary, Tonight the world was no longer awash with ash,
instead the sun lolled longer, peeling kisses from her lips like orange rinds.

vii

This worm-juicy symphony! Sweat and spit stir and slip,
inviting the dirt's lips to split. The shrill agendas of alcoholics surround us.

I meet a seventy-year-old Jewish woman named Margot who survived Auschwitz
and fertility experiments — what will the spring flowers say to her this year?

Pussy willows open their tattered pocketbooks like aristocrats escaping
who produce heirlooms at dawn and beg the border guards for political asylum.

Floorboards creak all night long in our house; the ghosts must go soon,
all night they tremble and fold their secrets in the growing heat of the trees.

The mirror is smoke-colored, shadows flit across its surface like anxious squirrels.
Shark-eyed, the mirror says, "Unleash your opera."

And when I think of spring I think of love, I remember again
the night my roots exploded and mud sloshed in my guts.

O spring! Beautiful spring! How you resex the swinging trees
and sing our trembling skins to sleep.

Cape Cod

Houses live and die.

—T. S. Eliot

Inside everything was Episcopalian—
the wicker chaise lounges, the small spotted mirrors,
the rattan dining room set, the tears.
No one saw tears. We hid them—
especially the men, who buried their tears
in the sea, or so I once dreamed and wrote down,
until the dream became what I believed and what I wrote.
Our family owned a large house by the sea,
built in 1902, white as a hospital.
There was a wrap-around porch where old rockers rocked,
regardless of whether or not people rocked in them.
Martha's Vineyard winked from each room.
The island whispered: *I will be lovely, but never too close.*
Each bedroom was painted a different color—
green, pink, yellow, blue, red.
Corresponding gingham curtains and gingham bedspreads
inhaled and exhaled the sea, creating a refrain of sighs and regrets,
part of the rhythm of the place.
Our iron beds squeaked when we jumped in.
We read warped books filled with sand.
I don't remember that we talked much.
Why didn't we talk much?
The wainscoting downstairs was dark, shiny, smooth as church pews.
All the house's corners were obscure, not filled in.
The windows had two rows of small panes on top
and a large bottom sash with thick smoky glass

and so our vision was a curious combination of miniaturist boxes
and expansive cropped abstracted seascapes
that never could get enough of the world jammed into them,
but always there was distance, distance and occlusion.
Two staircases xylophoned with the steps
of guests, relatives, and summer help.
There was even a great-aunt who had sung for the Met —
her hair was dyed the color of champagne
and she had a nose job and a topaz amulet.
She was old, had married badly and embodied regret,
although she had known the love of crowds
which dragged behind her like a wedding train.
There was a yacht club meeting every summer
with a cannon that went off — *baboom!*
Women arrived in their thin Talbots belts,
carrying wicker purses shaped like paint cans
with whalebone carvings fastened on top,
resembling the hardened excrement seagulls drop.
Occasionally the purses would open,
albeit reluctantly, like safe-deposit boxes.
Men wore cranberry trousers and Brooks Brothers blue blazers.
The same nervous postures came with the martinis.
We all repeated the same orchestrated blocking.
Names grew few, more and more the same.
Those with sexual peculiarities hid,
which meant most of us hid.
The sea grass zithered somberly
and the *Rosa rugosa* filled in the background
with a red quivering, like eyes saddened or irritated,
held in check by pruned privet hedges
and the waves drew in, the waves drew out, in, out, in, out —
like a long important political speech
no one recalled but everyone knew.
Old station wagons came, went.
The beach stretched out in a long boomerang-arc
and the shoreline was speckled with dark purplish seaweed flecks —

an endless message written for someone.
Sometimes an enormous fog rolled in,
erasing the sea, the roads.
One year a neighbor killed herself.
Her husband returned the following summer
with a new wife who looked like the first wife,
only younger. Time passed. She grew old.
The yacht club meetings still continue
as far as I know, and often, at night,
in summer, the fireflies still grow dizzy,
or are they stars? Maybe both?
The station wagons still rattle down the sandy roads,
getting stuck in the dunes by drunk teens
lost to the tedium of love's small scale,
their inaccurate kisses drowned out by the sea
with its deeper secrets, the sea that shifts and advances
and undoes itself with whispers.
One September, after the season had ended,
an austere real estate agent appeared from Sotheby's,
opening our front door with his very own keys.
His gestures were rehearsed, yet chummy.
We were the dead
and the living had come to size us up.
Silver candlestick holders lay on the floor.
Photographs of people who looked a lot like us
were shoved into garbage bags.
The Massachusetts sky was small and cold.
Our house was sold.

Ponies

I remember the ponies in the distance.
I remember you talked of a war, no, two wars, a failed marriage —
discreetly, without force or grandeur.
This was before they amputated your leg, before the stroke.
You rolled your *r*'s, spoke of Oxford,
recalled driving in the Quaker ambulance unit in China,
where you saw an oil drum filled with severed limbs.
Pleased to have your approval, I rarely spoke.
You were like a father to me and I was grateful.
I remember the ponies behind the fence, muscular,
breathing, how they worried the grass.
The ponies said: *This day astounds us. The field is green.*
We love nothing better than space and more space.
Ah, they knew what I needed to know.
They lived in their bodies.
If the ponies wanted to kiss, they kissed.
They moved like the shadows of airplanes.
They knew no hatred, but fear they understood.
The sky was shot clear with blue.
After the picnic, we gathered the tablecloth.
As we left, I could still see the ponies,
crowding one another, free and unbroken.

Triptych

i. Politics

My mother canvasses for Nixon
among Angela Davis supporters.
Already she looks sad, strained,
trying to resemble Jackie Kennedy.
I am six. *The Ed Sullivan Show* is on.
Janis Joplin shakes with pain.
Already I know this ugly singer
from Port Arthur, Texas,
understands all my mother will endure.
What happened to my mother?
What disturbed her all her life?
One day she will say things to me.
She will call me an abomination.

ii. Homosexuality

After my mother and father fight,
my father takes my hand
and we walk down to the Mississippi
where he smokes Camel cigarettes.
He flicks his ashes away from me.
He rarely says my name.
All day on TV, I watch monks
in Saigon douse themselves in gasoline
and light their saffron robes on fire.
When they ignite, they do not cry out.
I study their silence to comprehend
how a tongue turns into flame.

iii. Easter

I am young. Six. Or seven.
My sweat does not smell.
I am not an angel, kicking
the can, playing doctor.
My father's drinking is bad.
He slurs his pandemonium
with the words God and Christ.
He bursts with perils, dooms
me with promises. Outside,
the Mississippi pushes faster,
forces its voice down the banks
of sumac, connecting tributaries
and creeks. My soul is now
deep and moves like the river.

Étude

Go to the gay bar where the young and old men flirt,
listen to their conversations, short and curt,
study the dance music thumping in your chest,
maybe mention how there is more of an emphasis
on anticipation as opposed to the event,
it might help you along a bit, if helping along is what you require,
a century has ended, a new one begins,
this small seaside city is done in faux-Tuscan,
note the overly made-up women in Chanel suits
nodding inside the banquettes of the fancy restaurants,
they wait as we all must wait,
smell the vias heavy with hibiscus, gardenias and grapettes,
this is America, this is Florida,
where history is rarely exact and the seduction of beauty is all,
feel the city gather on your skin—
the dirt, the exhaust, the laundry steam, the brine,
let the tip of your tongue taste the ruined domes
of the churches corroded by the Atlantic,
observe the windows reflecting the police cruisers
that go—red blue red blue red blue—
listen to the bombardier beetles strum their instruments,
see the lamps of the big estates brighten,
mark the stands of casuarina pines solidifying,
and if a new friend should take your arm
do not define the gesture, no,
let the moon spread her shampoo all over you,
allow the palm trees with their shallow roots
to lull you down the broad avenue.

Florida Ghazals

in memory of John Stephen Reece

i

Down here, the sun clings to the earth and there is no darkness.
Down here, the silence of the sea and the silence of the swamp seep into our muscles.

All night, Dolores labors between the sea grapes and the empty park.
Our town prostitute, she listens for a long time. Her listening makes her strong.

The teenage boy locks his door and combs the obscene magazine.
His callused left hand chops the gloss in waves. The silence of the naked ladies builds.

The Cape Sable seaside sparrows' population dropped 25 percent. Females are silent.
Male calls are counted and multiplied by sixteen: this is how we track what
    cannot be seen.

Gay waiters examine their haircuts in the mirrors.
Perhaps tonight their pursuit of love will end in some permanence?

Juan escapes from our prison; he duct-tapes *Playboy* magazines to his rib cage.
With his glossy carapace, he vaults over the razor strips of the chainlink fence.

Egas Moniz wins the Nobel Prize in 1949 for pioneering lobotomies.
I am a pioneer of silence but the silencing of madness haunts me because it is
    unresolved.

ii

The hairdresser measures his delicate architecture.
Do all of life's devotions dissolve at the shores of the day's ugly punches?

Dolores teases her blond hair a foot into the air, her hair the one perfection
in this low-income town, a conspicuous example of Darwinian sexual selection.

Consider the teenage boy again. His locked room is a diorama of loneliness.
He bucks his hips until his hurricanes of desire are arrested. Then comes a deep
    silence.

Weather. Weather. How's the weather?
When I speak of the weather is it because I cannot speak of my days spent in the
    nuthouse?

Juan sinks into the swamp thick with processed excrement.
Nude paper ladies sink him like cement, silencing him.

The men in the gym slow down their repetitions, their biceps grow; they are silent
    in their strength.
When does silence go from being an asset to a liability?

All this beauty. Butterflies at the ankles. Birds, birds.
When hurricanes come with their bad names, they ruin this place like madness.

iii

Elizabeth Bishop was five when her mother went mad.
They locked her mother away in Nova Scotia and Elizabeth never saw her again.

The men on death row are gathering in their silence, not unlike the Miccosukee
    tribal leaders
who sit in their thatched huts in the swamp and murmur over mistakes made.

The black prison guards shoot bullets into the dark and swear at Juan.
Their blue armpits open and close. They will not be satisfied with anything but silence.

Tonight the gym fills with strong male groans.
I am among these wordless men bent on increasing their size.

I keep vigil by the light of my 60-watt bulb.
The unmarked mass grave of the 1928 hurricane beckons me.

Long ago my cousin was murdered, drowned in a river in St. Augustine.
He was twenty-three years old. My aunt went mad. Now I speak for the dead.

In the summer, there is heat, silence and no people. This is the weather of poetry.
In the summer, it rains sideways, leaking through the roofs of our mouths.

When Elizabeth Bishop lived in Key West the sea breeze brushed her with peace.
This aquamarine sea, these royal palms assuaged her. So too with me.

Even at Christmas, hornets hiss in the kiss of the hibiscus.
Our seasons come upon us silently.

I hear Juan drown in the night, his mouth stuffed with rain.
The swamp water jiggles its razors at his throat.

When I come out at last from the dark I am committed.
I press my fingers on the keys. There are no more locked wards.

At dawn the pelican spears the sea spastically.
Down here, everything gushes with the phlegm of dependency.

Bethesda-by-the-Sea cools with the gossip of the dead.
The ministers attend to the living, inserting wafers like coins dropped into slot
    machines.

Florida is a frontier built by escapees.
We electrocute men. No one's past is certain.

v

Philomela held her cut tongue in her hand like a ticket.
Although her past was heavy, her silence strengthened her, gave her wings.

In Lantana, at night, the 1950s pink tubercular sanatorium glows with florescence.
Behind the dirty jalousie window slats, the AIDS patients play cards.

When I came to this place I had nothing of the past, no photo albums, nothing.
Silence is my ancestor.

That night my cousin must have been scared, surrounded by the muscles of men.
He must have fought back, he must have cried out. Or was he silent?

I press on the keys of the typewriter attempting to record all those lost and unmarked.
But there are too many, I cannot keep track.

The Haitian ladies throw back their regal heads and move down the sidewalks slow
as if they were on the deck of a ship taking them away from some awful place.

Alligators swallow the summer light. The thick grass eats the sidewalk.
Whatever is built here is quickly overrun with the advance of chlorophyll.

Robert Fitzroy, the father of weather forecasting, slit his throat with a razor.
Is it brooding on the future that drives us mad? The silence of it?

In a room, in an institution, I was. Behind me, a window with rain.
A chaplain attended me. We had nothing to share but silence.

Lantana, where I live, is home to the *National Enquirer.*
Their one-story locked headquarters resemble mental houses.

One year I lived in a Moorish hacienda, built in 1924. The walls were two feet thick.
My neighbor was a peeping Tom. At night his feet crushed the grass like a cat's paws.

In the bluish purple bruise of dawn, Dolores watches weather on TV channeled
    from a dish.
She lost her only son in Vietnam and now there can be no silence.

Waves open and close like doors between these islands called keys.
Sea horses shift in the shallows like coy Tiresiases and say: "Relax, everyone's
    bisexual."

At night I hear the electric chair whir.
Men who make terrible mistakes disappear here.

In the store there was a man who was more beautiful than his wife.
The man flirted with me, then showed a wallet, inside was a picture with children.

Easter in Palm Beach and at the Everglades Club the ladies sit before lemon tarts
on filigreed plates, their sprayed hair fastened on their heads like conch shells.

When the 1928 hurricane came it had no name.
Lake Okeechobee broke and 2,000 migrant workers drowned in their shacks.

It was dark and my cousin was alone. They dragged him to the river.
It rained for three days. They could not find him; when they did, no one knew his
       name.

In church we hear the jungle growing to meet the sea.
Each Sunday we remember the dead in silence, but it is not enough.

Florida has no memory besides the monarch butterflies who remember everything.
The sea glitters, fish disappear like keys. O, this land of exits. This land of
       forgetfulness.

When the last day of summer comes, the locals walk home wistful, discounted.
Down here, the lonely claim my voice and make it strong.

Interior

The jewelry shop is a small stage.
The very rich enter and exit
like actors in a Beckett play.
The salesman fills the bowl of nuts.
The bell rings, the door opens.
He smiles and will not be grim.
He talks of rubies, pearls, and clasps.
The day roars, speeds past him,
splinters light apricot shards
that fleck the man's cheeks.
The phone before him persists.
On his desk with brass handles,
a framed photo of Princess Diana,
who used to wear these jewels.
Today there's a bit of gossip
about a certain dissolute grandee.
Each day there is new traffic.
It is hard to recall who is who.
The old single female manager
coughs in spasms, steals sales,
ruminates over her childless state
and orders the salesman around.
Each day he forgives her anew.
As the light leaves the window,
he surveys all the silver objects
he will soon be asked to polish.
The tired man forgets and remembers
in equal proportions as he drinks
his last cup of bitter black coffee.

Addresses

i. To You

because I am moved because I shake and am bound
because I am matched to the city as well as the trees
because there is a stillness to the acres left I love
because I love the city's multiple doors left open
I stake my claim I swing my right hand up and down

I sing sacredly of suitcases and disappearances
I am a hymnal of my own making recording years
years that are empty years that are full
my eyes indicate some of my liberators failed
but there is no more time to speak of hurts

our time together is leached of extravagances
the room where I address you is empty at last
I open a big book I announce my name
the construction of leaves occupies my time
silence makes up the bulk of my estate

I am ruined but I am not afraid
the sound of the last empty lots is in my spine
from state to state I send out my report
I open my door I extend my hand
welcome

ii. Divinity Avenue

it is a dead end you know
they fail to mention that
from near and far we came
transvestites Buddhists
nuns ex-cons and myself
we stood with suitcases
below that yellow sign
we found rooms shelves
we unpacked crucifixes
photographs of the people
who inhabited our first house
in my room silence built
I took my right hand
smoothed a bible page
the bible's spine cracked
like the back of a butterfly
here I sat at a desk
finally without a tremor

iii. To My Brother

the postman circles with his thick blue sack
a school bus streaks the horizon with orange
carrying with it the shrieks of adolescents

someone is being teased someone is imitating
what it is like to be retarded to be handicapped
someone is shoved for being a homosexual

down the street the AA meeting starts up
in a church basement a coffee urn thumps
a wounded chorus unfolds their metal chairs

a retired stewardess with thick red lipstick
speaks of her umpteenth hospitalization
the clock empties its chest of sixty more ticks

another year passes still no word from you

iv. Pentimento

farther down the road is where I lived
an old farmhouse that creaked like a stage set
reverently I lived atop that hill overlooking that lake
most of the landscape was unfinished then still wet
hungry deer investigated the trees that whispered like crucifixes
I was forced to leave I was never the same
lately the housing developments have leveled everything
long ago I left and when I left I left with tears

v. Coda

this is the day I leave
leave the landscape I love
the way lovers love love
watch me how I leave
I have begun to shake
the hours are fleet
yet expansive as at death
I pack one suitcase
the lake plashes and hacks
Canada geese subtract
their gossip from the field
deer evacuate the sumac
their rough thick tongues
sandpaper the distances
they say *Don't look back*
I leave I look back

vi. United Hospital

the chaplain's name was Miss Grace
when she sat and talked to me
her shadow bled winged out
a map of a country I had not noticed
outside it was summer
the sky endless a glassed-off beautiful Bermuda blue
the day was a sea I could no longer swim in
the city of St. Paul loomed in the distance
apartment buildings mansions office buildings
impregnable as rows of tombstones
we were removed from the hullabaloo
Miss Grace had a talent for talk
she knew how to throw and mold paragraphs like pots
she had a knack for wedding and funeral soft-talk
she was an aristocrat in an Italian villa
her talk measured demonstrative
outside the day stayed blue so long
it amazed us with its endurance
Miss Grace blessed me with holy water
and always promised to return

vii. Blue

a November snow falls
blanking out the window wells
we sit in a basement apartment
deep in dark Minneapolis

the President has just been shot
his wife exits blood on her skirt
the nation is vast it obscures much
my father wears a blue thin tie

and sports a crew cut my mother
is crying again why does she cry
so much I am small but not afraid
a war begins but it is a mistake

I know this I know this
because I am a mistake

viii. To Those Grown Mute

it is dawn on the locked unit
the moon wheelbarrows her orchestra away
in the town the children are out of reach
my roommate's face is a peach that rots
the correct report of who I am disperses
the bank clerk who went off Lithium to have her first baby
has a brain that will not work
she lies on her bed like a snail without a house
the slits on her wrists itch
the nurse applies her lipstick behind her plate-glass station
her question is always the same
How will you get back
I move my rosary up and down in my right hand
the windows grow blue then clear as mirrors
we are all ambassadors carrying suitcases

ix. Fugue

Ye have not chosen me, but I have chosen you.

—John 15:16

our parents drink gin and sink into their state
Peter Paul and Mary sing the song about the jet plane

I am eight and afraid in our first house
together we hide and wait

you are an ambassador of silence
little brother still in your cribbed estate

adopted at birth your father was a teenager
blown to bits by the Vietcong

mother and father shake and swing the doors shut
a social worker comes and raises her right hand

writing her report but it is too late
the fighting begins I cross my hands

place my arms over my head
brother go back leave never come home

x. To Martha My Nurse

I leave the open unit and I am not afraid
I rent a room with a few flies
there is no sea for me to see
only these wheat fields beat by the sun

I had hoped for the sea but no
the sun shines on the gray cat
who purrs on the steamer trunk
you have sent me on my way

the hospital floats in the city like a yacht
this new room is bright yellow
I nail a crucifix upon one wall
the crucifix is from Latin America

a white Christ embraced by orange
the Christ says *Believe in me*
it is nearly two in the afternoon
there is much to do much to see

xi. Minneapolis

for Ann Young

young maples bordered the sidewalks
their tender leaves whispered of commitment
the Basilica of St. Mary's was the city's one extravagance
the rest was masculine and clean
in the bar the gay men cultivated their haircuts
arranging individual strands in the mirrors
like topiary experts often more than they cared to admit
these men who came from the farms in the Dakotas
had asked to escape
but the time to speak of hurts had passed
the time to speak of mistakes had passed
it was time to embrace the mistakes
it was time to dance with joy
the Mississippi glittered and listened
the skyscrapers cooled and listened

xii. Beverly Road

I still remember your house
on one wall a Key West pastel a house I knew
there was coffee from Amsterdam
a list of things to do
did you do them
the pine mantel bought on a lark
placed against a wall without a fireplace
there was something theatrical there
an extravagance all your own
didn't you light votive candles
all over the house before I came
like a monk late for vespers
candlelight against your temple
we talked the talk of predator and innocent
the city of St. Paul did not exist the sky retreated
there were no angels no ascensions
it felt like grace but it wasn't
we blessed each other as best we could
you never stayed in touch
although you promised you would

xiii. Afton

the day I leave Minnesota I am not afraid
after all the years and ghosts I am done
you can be done with a place
I am visiting a friend's house in the country

it is late fall almost winter my favorite time
dried white hydrangeas are on the windowsill
winds shove the house and whisper of failure
the hydrangeas shift in their pitcher like wigs

children pom-pom-pullaway on a faraway lawn
lost in their melancholy echolalia
the oak grove in the distance grows porous
and orange then ocher then charcoal

acquiring the dark like a sponge
such is life in the provinces
a drone storms me aimless in his masculinity
in the mirror I register what hair I've lost

in my right hand I hold a key
my legacy is to leave the room empty

xiv. Two Bright Rooms

on my birthday

Lantana is where I found two bright rooms
most forgotten of all South Florida towns
famous for fast food famous for low rents

next door a German shepherd pads in the heat
chained to his chain behind a chainlink fence
listen to his tongue crack on the concrete

a freight train shakes my dinner plate
across the street under the yellow-tab tree
the man without legs scratches his stumps

it is not Paris it is not Florence
but it has majesty in its anonymity
this town where people stop for gas

on their way to somewhere else
humidity cakes my skin
lamps light the specks on my terrazzo floor

all that remains unnoticed I adore
to the used furniture to the broken door
to the jalousie window slats I sing

hey nonny-nonny no hey nonny-nonny ney

xv. Boca Raton

Don't hurry the journey.

— C. P. Cavafy

I work in a crowd beneath a clock
everywhere I look a gated community
but anonymity is at home on me

a wedding band taps the counter
I wrap goods in soft tissue and say
Thank you very much please come back

in the back room the tailors stitch
cramped over their sewing machines
Isabella from Venezuela squints

thinking of dinner sweating praying
how many times has she done this act
who among the crowd knows her name

the manager stands next to me
he frets over a promotion he did not get
he tells me everything is politics

he tells me there are dress shirts to pin
these new cashmere sweaters to sell
I will never return to my first house

xvi. Loxahatchee

for John and Dorothy Harte

across an expanse of hot algae a great white heron flies
the borders of the Everglades shifted again last night
but I felt only the slightest tremor in my sleep
here in this swamp with the beautiful Indian name
I listen to the thousand thousand vows this world has made then broken

xvii. Summerland Key

down here history is made
in proportion to the amount of silence lost

the gumbo limbo tree generates its thin orange skin
each sheaf a vulnerable diary entry

in 1970 I knew each empty space now fenced
casuarina pines grew thick as walls

no one knew where one lot began where another ended
how did the island come to have no room

who ruined it with deeds
house after house and all the butterflies and parrotfish gone

did they go elsewhere or simply disappear
I am a part of this fractured frontier

xviii. Worth Avenue

one of the tailors the older one
whispers Maria Rizzatti makes mistakes
this morning a black ball gown slips from her hands
spills from her digits like the shadow of her estranged husband
the dark dark bits against her Latin hand
and not unlike something by Caravaggio
her callused fingers dive and mate
the store opens in ten minutes
Maria Rizzatti clutches her black disaster
as if it were the head of a thief
they will not fire her not yet
two sales clerks adjust each other's ties
the bells of Bethesda-by-the-Sea mark the hour
bong bong bong they go on and on bong bong bong
Maria Rizzatti thinks of Bogotá
a teenage love she had there once long ago

xix. I Have Dreamed of You So Much

that I am no longer who I once was
the room where I sleep has altered
from still life with hibiscus to an abstraction
it is not clear where I end and the dark starts
the town does a slow fade
the black men chum their bait over the bridge
their fishing lines cobweb the Atlantic
the train slows on its antique tracks
the sapphire-violet sea deepens and shushes
beneath the waves sea horses mate
changing their sex as they please
converting androgyny to energy like Christ

xx. Vizcaya

when you come as I hope you will soon we will go
the high-ceilinged rooms are appointed with life and death
we will listen to the guide and pay no attention ho-hum
however our distracted reverence will be enough
James Deering's ghost is generous to strangers
he who spent eight bachelor winters here long ago

the main gardens will be too much but we will inspect
our destiny depends upon a place so why not this one
it may very well be our last time together
life speeds up life stops abruptly as I know you know
I have brought you here to put you at ease and let you rest
I have very little left to say my energies flag

the adherence to schedules and connections taxes
I have brought you this far and when you see the spectacular collections
the rooms lavish with neoclassical beds slept and unslept in
you will understand at last what I have been trying to do
by the time you come I will have gone
Biscayne Bay tilts to your right like an Italian plate

everything has worked out nothing has come your way
but it is all here at Vizcaya I assure you of that much
the hammock forests you come to first will cover you
it will be dark at first so many leaves some rain and then O then
jets from a sarcophagus fountain the limestone sea horses
the drama of interiors frozen and moving you will see

the courtyards tea rooms libraries loggias and breakfast rooms
the old Cuban tiles the Irish fireplace the Roman columns
the shaped grass plots in the French style to live and die in
I have come this far to show you copper-latticed gazebos
at Vizcaya the spaces are full yet absent
I want to be there to see the sun on your face

if only we could stay here forever you might say
but no of course we must not linger
this is the scene of what becomes of love when it is done
mark it carefully you will not see it often
Minerva Neptune and Apollo wait for you under the banyans
trust me when I say your exquisite journey to Vizcaya awaits

Interlude

We are two men on a park bench
in Palm Beach oblivious to the two men

who start their truck with that boy
from the bar inside dragging him

in the dark to the fence strapping him
with a rope to a post in Laramie,

Wyoming, where he freezes and dies
over five days. My dear, it is late.

The Flagler Museum is shut.
Stay with me. Remain here with me.

Morbidezza

You leave the back door wide open,
    your bare feet thudding against the dirt,
the dirt cracked with hairy-fisted shoots,
    pummeling their messages skyward.

You walk straight into the garden
    wild with jetting juiced stalks.
You listen to the bees' talk harden.
    Pines swish their wrists, discarding needles

like clock hands. It is 4 P.M.; the garden's edges brown.
    The clouds drop; the sky goes blueberry blue.
You hear the night push her plausive voice,
    glistering with perfumeries.

You rush back in, clutching a bouquet of irises,
    the crumbling farmhouse blushing with dusk.
You place the irises in a vase on the hutch. The irises' beards
    purple and sweat while you go off to sleep,

your gorgeous middle-aged torso yielding,
    your nostrils drumming like dove chests.
Have I added too many strokes? I want so much
    to make you real, to get it right.

Bread Loaf and the Bakeless Prizes

The Katharine Bakeless Nason Literary Publication Prizes were established in 1995 to expand the Bread Loaf Writers' Conference's commitment to the support of emerging writers. Endowed by the LZ Francis Foundation, the prizes commemorate Middlebury College patron Katharine Bakeless Nason and launch the publication career of a poet, a fiction writer, and a creative-nonfiction writer annually. Winning manuscripts are chosen in an open national competition by a distinguished judge in each genre. Winners are published by Houghton Mifflin Company in Mariner paperback original.

JUDGES FOR 2003:

Louise Glück, poetry

Jay Parini, fiction

Ted Conover, creative nonfiction